CHICAGO

CUBS

BY ANTHONY K. HEWSON

SportsZone

An Imprint of Abdo Publishing
abdobooks.com

abdobooks.com

Published by Abdo Publishing, a division of ABDO, PO Box 398166, Minneapolis, Minnesota 55439. Copyright © 2023 by Abdo Consulting Group, Inc. International copyrights reserved in all countries. No part of this book may be reproduced in any form without written permission from the publisher. SportsZone™ is a trademark and logo of Abdo Publishing.

Printed in the United States of America, North Mankato, Minnesota.
102022
012023

THIS BOOK CONTAINS
RECYCLED MATERIALS

Cover Photo: Todd Kirkland/Getty Images Sport/Getty Images
Interior Photos: Tim Bradbury/Getty Images Sport/Getty Images, 4; Picture Now/
Universal Images Group/Getty Images, 7; Bruce Bennett Studios/Getty Images Studios/
Getty Images, 9; FPG/Archive Photos/Getty Images, 11; Transcendental Graphics/Archive
Photos/Getty Images, 12; Joseph Aaron Campbell/Chicago History Museum/Getty
Images, 15; Library of Congress/Corbis Historical/VCG/Getty Images, 17; Bettmann/Getty
Images, 19, 23; Chicago Daily News Inc./Chicago History Museum/Getty Images, 20; MLB
Photos/Hulton Archive/Getty Images, 25; Ron Vesely/MLB Photos/Getty Images Sport/
Getty Images, 27; Jonathan Daniel/Getty Images Sport/Getty Images, 29, 32; Beth A.
Keiser/AP Images, 31; Amy Sancetta/AP Images, 34; Mark J. Terrill/AP Images, 37; Nick
Cammett/Diamond Images/Getty Images, 38; Kyodo/AP Images, 39; Joe Robbins/Icon
Sportswire/Getty Images, 41

Editor: Charlie Beattie
Series Designer: Becky Daum

Library of Congress Control Number: 2022940395

Publisher's Cataloging-in-Publication Data

Names: Hewson, Anthony K., author.
Title: Chicago Cubs / by Anthony K. Hewson
Description: Minneapolis, Minnesota: Abdo Publishing, 2023 | Series: Inside MLB |
     Includes online resources and index.
Identifiers: ISBN 9781098290122 (lib. bdg.) | ISBN 9781098275327 (ebook)
Subjects: LCSH: Chicago Cubs (Baseball team) --Juvenile literature. | Baseball
     teams--Juvenile literature. | Professional sports--Juvenile literature. | Sports
     franchises--Juvenile literature. | Major League Baseball (Organization)--Juvenile
     literature.
Classification: DDC 796.35764--dc23

TABLE OF

CONTENTS

CHAPTER 1

THE LONG WAIT

When the 2016 World Series began, baseball fans knew they were about to witness the end of a long drought. The Chicago Cubs had been waiting 108 years for a championship. Their opponents, the Cleveland Indians, had not won since 1948. As if the teams hadn't already waited long enough, the series then went the maximum seven games. Then an eighth-inning three-run Cleveland rally sent Game 7 to extra innings. And then the sky opened up.

Rain poured down on Cleveland's Progressive Field. Players had to wait in the dugout, not knowing when the game would resume. As the Cubs sat, teammate Jason Heyward got their

Veteran outfielder Jason Heyward was in his first year with the Cubs in 2016.

attention. The veteran outfielder called them into a small room near the dugout.

None of the other players knew what Heyward was going to say. Meanwhile, Cubs fans around the world were wondering if the late collapse meant Chicago's misery would continue for another year. The players felt the weight of the streak holding them down. Heyward wanted to pick everyone back up.

"We're the best team in baseball," Heyward said. "And we're the best team in baseball for a reason. Now we're going to show it."

WHITE STOCKINGS, COLTS, AND ORPHANS

Over a century before Heyward gave his speech, the Cubs met the Chicago White Sox in one of the first World Series. The matchup, in 1906, was the start of a long crosstown rivalry between the two teams. But 30 years earlier, when the Cubs were founded, they were the ones named after white socks.

The Cubs debuted as the Chicago White Stockings in 1876. That year they won the first-ever National League (NL) title. Chicago went 52–14 and led the league in almost every offensive category. In the days before the World Series, winning the NL title was the top prize in all of baseball.

The White Stockings had some of the best players in the game. But Chicago's biggest star was third baseman Adrian

"Cap" Anson. One of the best hitters of his day, Anson was an instant success in Chicago when he arrived in 1876. He spent 22 of his 27 professional seasons in Chicago and became the first member of baseball's 3,000-hit club in 1897. Over the next 121 years, only 31 players joined him. Between 1880 and 1891, he led the NL in runs batted in (RBIs) eight times. He did all of this while serving as Chicago's manager, a role he held for 19 seasons.

Cap Anson was elected to the Baseball Hall of Fame in 1939.

Anson led Chicago to four titles in the first seven NL seasons. They won again in 1885 and 1886. The only rival league to the NL in those days was the American Association (AA). In an early version of the World Series, the White Stockings met the AA champions, the St. Louis Browns, both years. The 1885 series ended in a tie. In 1886 St. Louis won in

ANSON'S REGRETTABLE HISTORY

Cap Anson was certainly a skillful player on the field. But he was far from a model off it. On multiple occasions in the 1880s, Anson refused to have his White Stockings compete against teams that fielded Black players. His actions helped lead baseball owners to informally ban Black players in the late 1800s. The ban stood until 1947.

six games. It was the beginning of a long baseball rivalry between the two cities.

Soon after, the White Stockings entered a period of decline. The team turned to younger players. Because of this, the team picked up "Colts" as a new nickname. Only Anson remained, but he was fired as manager and released as a player in 1897. Without the man who had guided the team for so long, people began calling Chicago the "Orphans."

A RIVAL MOVES IN

The team didn't just change names often in its early years. It also moved around quite a bit. By 1899 the club had settled in West Side Grounds on the west side of Chicago. The team had previously played at several ballparks around the city, including one year at South Side Park. In 1899 Orphans president James Hart allowed a team from the American League (AL) to move into the south side of the city. The new team had just relocated from St. Paul, Minnesota. The AL at the time was a minor league, not on the level of the NL. Hart didn't consider them a rival.

However, by 1901, that had changed. The AL became a major league right alongside the NL. The Orphans began losing players to this new team. The new club also picked up the nickname White Stockings that the Orphans had abandoned years earlier. That team today is known as the Chicago White Sox.

Shortstop Joe Tinker, *left*, and second baseman Johnny Evers, *right*, were a famous double-play combination for the Cubs in the early 1900s.

Chicago's new AL team was successful right away. And the Orphans were still struggling in the standings. But improvement was not far away.

HERE COME THE CUBS

In 1902 the Orphans again featured a young roster. This led to a new nickname—"Cubs." It took a few years for the name to catch on, and it wasn't official until 1907. But the team has commonly been known as the Cubs since 1903.

TINKER TO EVERS TO CHANCE

The Cubs' infield combination of Joe Tinker, Johnny Evers, and Frank Chance inspired *New York Evening Mail* writer Franklin P. Adams to pen a famous poem about their double-play abilities. It read: "These are the saddest of possible words / Tinker to Evers to Chance / Trio of bear cubs / Fleeter than birds / Tinker to Evers to Chance / Ruthlessly pricking our gonfalon bubble / Making a Giant hit into a double / Words that are heavy with nothing but trouble / Tinker to Evers to Chance."

Those Cubs grew up in a hurry. The team was loaded with future Hall of Famers, including most of its infield. Shortstop Joe Tinker, second baseman Johnny Evers, and first baseman Frank Chance turned potential hits into outs for a decade together.

Pitcher Mordecai "Three Finger" Brown was the team's ace. As a young man, he had lost most of his right index finger in a farming accident. Hitters believed that was the key to his success. Brown was able to manipulate the ball in a way that no other pitcher could.

These players helped the Cubs return to the top of the NL mountain and win the title in 1906. With the rise of the AL as a major league, the AL and NL champions began facing off in the World Series in 1903. In the Cubs' first World Series, they drew their new rival, the White Sox.

The Cubs were baseball's dominant team that year. They won a record 116 games. By contrast, the White Sox were the

Mordecai "Three Finger" Brown set a Cubs record with a 1.04 earned run average in 1906.

worst-hitting team in the AL. Their .230 team batting average earned them the nickname "Hitless Wonders."

The Sox did hit very poorly in the World Series, just .198 as a team. But that was better than the Cubs, who hit .196 against a sturdy White Sox pitching staff. The Sox finally exploded for eight runs in Game 5 to take a 3–2 series lead. Needing a win to survive, the Cubs sent Brown out to start Game 6. But the righty had just pitched a complete game two days earlier. The White Sox thumped him for seven runs in the first two innings. An 8–3 Cubs loss completed the White Sox upset. But both Brown and the Cubs would get a shot at redemption soon.

THE NORTH SIDE NINE

In 1907 the Cubs once again won more than 100 games. Mordecai Brown led a dominant pitching staff. The Cubs crushed the rest of the NL on their way back to the World Series. This time Chicago faced the Detroit Tigers and their legendary right fielder Ty Cobb.

In Game 1, the teams were still tied 3–3 after 12 innings. In those days, ballparks did not have lights. When it became too dark to keep playing, umpires often declared games over. Those games ended in ties.

Chicago's pitchers dominated the rest of the series, allowing just three total runs in four straight wins. Cobb hit just 4-for-20.

Frank Chance managed the Cubs to World Series titles in 1907 and 1908 while also serving as the team's first baseman.

Brown started Game 5 and shut out the Tigers to clinch the Cubs' first World Series title.

The two teams met again in the 1908 World Series. But this time it took some dramatic events for Chicago to get there.

The Cubs dueled with the New York Giants for first place all season long. In late September, the teams met for a huge series in New York. The Cubs won the first two games. On September 23, the third game was tied in the bottom of the ninth. The Giants appeared to get the game-winning hit. Fans stormed onto the field to celebrate. The Giants' Fred Merkle, who had been running from first to second, trotted off the field. But the Cubs noticed Merkle never touched second base.

Johnny Evers scrambled through the crowd to find the ball, then raced to tag second. Merkle was called out. The game wasn't over. But with so many fans on the field, the umpires had to call it off. The game was replayed on October 8. Both teams were tied for first place. The Cubs won the rematch 4–2 and went back to the World Series.

Brown won a Cubs-record 29 games in 1908. He also won two World Series games, including a shutout in Game 4. After a 2–0 win in Game 5, the Cubs became the first team ever to win back-to-back World Series.

In those days, there were no playoffs. The first-place team from each league went right to the World Series. Several great clubs missed out altogether. Despite winning 104 games in 1909, the Cubs finished second in the NL. They made it back to the World Series in 1910 but lost in five games to the Philadelphia Athletics.

Even Frank Schulte, the first NL Most Valuable Player (MVP) winner in Cubs history, couldn't lift the team above second place in 1911. No one knew at the time that the Cubs' wait for another title would last for more than a century.

THE WRIGLEY YEARS

A pair of important figures in Cubs history joined the organization in 1916. A new group of owners bought the

Frank "Wildfire" Schulte had 30 doubles, 21 triples, 21 home runs, and 23 stolen bases in his MVP season of 1911.

team that year. One of them was Charles Weeghman. Among his first acts was to move the team into the stadium he owned, Weeghman Park, on Chicago's north side.

WANDERING CUBS

The Cubs had six different home fields from 1876 to 1916. Their longest stay was at West Side Grounds, roughly 10 miles (16.1 km) south of Wrigley Field, for 22 full seasons. They also had their most success there as they won two World Series.

Another owner was chewing-gum manufacturer William Wrigley. He gradually took on a larger share of the Cubs and bought up Weeghman's shares in 1918.

That same year, the Cubs made another World Series run. Chicago faced the Boston Red Sox. Before he became baseball's home run king, Babe Ruth was a talented young Boston pitcher. And he won two games against the Cubs to help the Red Sox take the series 4–2.

Wrigley changed the name of the stadium from Weeghman Park to Cubs Park. He eventually put his own name on the building after the 1926 season. The ballpark has been called Wrigley Field ever since.

THE COLLAPSE AND THE CALLED SHOT

The NL was a tough league to beat in the 1920s. Despite consistent winning seasons, the Cubs rarely rose above fourth place. That changed in 1929, when Chicago blasted its way back to the World Series.

The team was led by a slew of Hall of Famers. Slugging center fielder Lewis "Hack" Wilson stood only 5 feet, 6 inches

Hack Wilson, *left,* Rogers Hornsby, *center,* and Kiki Cuyler, *right,* all hit .345 or better for the Cubs in 1929.

tall, but he had tremendous power. Wilson led the major leagues with 159 RBIs. Second baseman Rogers Hornsby was one of the best hitters of his era. His .380 batting average topped the team as he was named NL MVP. Speedy outfielder Kiki Cuyler stole a team-high 43 bases. Together they helped Chicago win the NL by 10 1/2 games. That set up a showdown with the powerful Philadelphia Athletics in the World Series.

The Cubs' big bats went quiet in the first three games, scoring only five runs. Still, Chicago won Game 3. And when the Cubs jumped out to an 8–0 lead in Game 4, they looked to be back on track. But Philadelphia teed off on Cubs starter Charlie Root in the seventh inning. The A's scored six runs to knock him from the game. Then they added four more in the inning off two Cubs relievers for a stunning 10–8 victory. The rattled Cubs folded in Game 5 as the Athletics claimed the title.

Chicago won the NL again in 1932. One World Series opponent was a familiar one. Fourteen years after the Cubs were shut down by Babe Ruth the pitcher, they faced Babe Ruth the slugger, now with the New York Yankees.

Already trailing 2–0 in the series, the Cubs returned home for Game 3. Ruth quickly put the Yankees on top with a three-run blast in the first. Chicago fans and players then began hurling insults at Ruth. The heckling was still going on when he came back up to bat in the fifth.

Ruth responded by pointing somewhere on the field. To this day it is debated whether he was pointing at the first-base stands, the Cubs' dugout, or the outfield. But he then blasted Root's next pitch for a home run to deep center. Ruth's hotly debated "called shot" became a legendary moment in his career and baseball history. The Yankees went on to win the series in four games.

HACK RACKS UP RBIs

In 1930 Hack Wilson plowed through pitchers and set a Major League Baseball (MLB) record with 191 RBIs. The record is considered one of the most unbreakable in baseball. Only two other players have topped 180. And since 1938, only one player, Cleveland's Manny Ramirez in 1999, has come within 26 of Wilson's mark.

NO TAMING THE TIGERS

William Wrigley never saw the Cubs fall in the 1932 World Series. He had died before the season. Ownership of the team passed to his son, Philip, known as P. K.

Gabby Hartnett was the first MLB catcher ever to hit more than 20 home runs in a season.

On the field, not much changed at first. The Cubs returned to the World Series in 1935. Wilson, Cuyler, and Hornsby were all gone. But the Cubs still had veteran Gabby Hartnett to lead the way. The slugging catcher was in his 14th season in 1935. But he won his only career MVP Award that year after hitting .344.

The Cubs met their old AL rivals, the Tigers, in the World Series. After five games, Chicago trailed 3–2. Game 6 in Detroit was tied 3–3 going into the ninth inning. Chicago third baseman Stan Hack led off with a triple. But the rest of the Cubs failed to drive him in. The Tigers then broke Cubs fans' hearts with a two-out, run-scoring single in the bottom of the ninth.

CHAPTER 3

THE LOVABLE LOSERS

Some longtime Cubs traditions first took shape in 1937. In July, construction began on the outfield bleachers and scoreboard at Wrigley Field. The scoreboard is still hand-operated today as it was then. That September, team president Bill Veeck had the idea to grow ivy on the brick outfield walls. The lush vine that turns bright green in the summer is now an iconic symbol of Wrigley Field.

In 1938 the Cubs spent much of the season chasing the Pittsburgh Pirates for the NL title. On September 28, the teams met in Chicago with the Cubs trailing Pittsburgh by a half game. Twice the Cubs rallied from two-run deficits. The game stood 5–5 heading to the bottom of the ninth inning.

A crowd mobs Cubs catcher Gabby Hartnett after he hit his dramatic walk-off home run against the Pittsburgh Pirates on September 28, 1938.

FLY THE W

In 1937 fans couldn't check online to see whether the Cubs won. To let fans know, that year the Cubs began raising flags above the scoreboard that gave the result of that day's game. A white flag with a blue W meant the Cubs won. A blue flag with a white L meant they lost. The flags are still flown today.

However, darkness was creeping across Wrigley Field as the game went later and later. The umpires had already ruled the game would not continue into a 10th inning. Gabby Hartnett, now 37 years old, remained the team's star catcher. And when he stepped up with two outs and ripped a game-winning homer, the Cubs moved into first place.

Hartnett's homer was dubbed "the Homer in the Gloamin'." The legendary hit helped propel the Cubs back to the World Series. They met the mighty Yankees. Once again, they were no match for the AL champions. New York swept the series, Chicago's fourth loss in 10 years.

THE CURSE OF THE BILLY GOAT

In 1945 the Cubs jumped from fourth place the year before to NL champions. First baseman Phil Cavarretta hit .355 and was named NL MVP.

The surprise season set up another World Series meeting with the Detroit Tigers. The Cubs came out swinging and thumped Detroit 9–0 in Game 1. The teams then split the next two as the series shifted back to Chicago.

First baseman Phil Cavarretta led the Cubs to the 1945 National League pennant and hit .423 in the World Series against Detroit.

Local bar owner William Sianis tried to attend Game 4 with an unusual companion—his pet goat, Murphy. The goat was not allowed to enter the park. Sianis was so insulted that he reportedly "cursed" the team, saying the Cubs would never win the World Series again.

Chicago went on to lose Games 4 and 5. A dramatic, 12-inning victory in Game 6 kept the Cubs alive. But they fell flat in Game 7. Detroit scored five first-inning runs on its way to a 9–3 win. It was a seventh straight World Series loss for Chicago. And "the Curse of the Billy Goat" was born.

MR. CUB

From 1946 to 1983, the Cubs didn't play in a single playoff game. They didn't even have a winning record from 1947 to 1962. However, during those struggles came some of the team's most beloved players.

Before 1947, Black players had been banned from MLB by team owners. But after Jackie Robinson debuted with the Brooklyn Dodgers, MLB teams soon signed other Black stars. Chicago brought in former Negro League standout Ernie Banks. The shortstop went on to win two NL MVP Awards. Later in his career, he moved to first base and continued slugging home runs. He ended his career in 1971 having reached 512 dingers.

Even more notable than Banks's ability was his enthusiasm for baseball. He was often quoted as saying, "It's a great day for baseball. Let's play two!" Banks remains such a legend in Chicago that his nickname is simply "Mr. Cub."

Ernie Banks played 2,528 games in a Cubs uniform, a club record.

Ron Santo spent all but one of his professional seasons on Chicago's north side. He joined the team in 1960 and became a nine-time All Star at third base. After he retired, Santo became a popular analyst on Cubs radio broadcasts until his death in 2010.

One of the most memorable seasons of this era came in 1969. It was Banks's final All-Star season. Santo pitched in 29 home runs. Meanwhile, ace pitcher Ferguson Jenkins led the staff as the Cubs comfortably led the NL East for most of the season. However, the team's "curse" seemed to pop up again in September. As the team faced the eventual World Series champion New York Mets, a black cat walked in front of Santo while he was warming up in the batters' box. The Mets swept the series on their way to a convincing division title.

MORE HEARTBREAK

In 1981 the Cubs were sold to the Tribune Company, which owned the *Chicago Tribune* newspaper. The sale ended 60 years of Wrigley family ownership.

The new owners inherited a team that had picked up an unfortunate nickname. Years of failure had not made the Cubs any less popular with fans. But those who crowded into Wrigley Field now called the Cubs "Loveable Losers."

Chicago second baseman Ryne Sandberg was an All-Star every year from 1984 to 1993.

Dallas Green was brought in as Chicago's new general manager. Green had previously worked for the 1980 World Series champion Philadelphia Phillies. One of the first moves he made was to trade for Ryne Sandberg. The second baseman kicked off a Hall-of-Fame career when he came to Chicago.

And by 1984, Green's other deals helped make the Cubs a winning team.

That year the Cubs won the NL East by 6 1/2 games. Pitcher Rick Sutcliffe won the Cy Young Award, and Sandberg was MVP. They rolled into the best-of-five NL Championship Series (NLCS) against the underdog San Diego Padres. The Cubs took a 2–0 lead, but then Chicago's history of misfortune showed up again.

In a tied Game 4, closer Lee Smith allowed a two-run game-winning home run to Padres first baseman Steve Garvey. The Cubs then took a 3–2 lead into the seventh inning of the decisive Game 5. But the Padres scored four runs after Chicago first baseman Leon Durham botched a routine ground ball. San Diego closed out the series with a 6–3 win.

By 1989 the Cubs had added slugging outfielder Andre Dawson. He paced the offense along with Sandberg and first baseman Mark Grace. Sutcliffe and young right-hander Greg Maddux led the pitching staff. The Cubs finished 93–69.

LET THERE BE LIGHT

The Cubs have historically played mostly day games. Until 1988 Wrigley Field did not even have lights. But even with lights installed, the Cubs still play most of their Friday, Saturday, and Sunday home games during the day.

Broadcaster Harry Caray leads Cubs fans in singing "Take Me Out to the Ball Game" during a game at Wrigley Field in 1996.

But in the NLCS, the Cubs were blown away 4–1 by the San Francisco Giants. Chicago lost leads in each of the last three games.

SUMMER OF '98

One of the first hires the Tribune Company made after taking over was a new television broadcaster. Harry Caray had been a baseball play-by-play man since 1945 with several different teams. In 1982 he left the Chicago White Sox and came to the north side. Almost immediately he became a Cubs legend.

Caray's boisterous personality spread to the fans. He was known for shouting "Holy Cow!" when his team hit a home run. And he openly rooted for the Cubs on the air. One of Caray's most famous routines was leading the crowd in the traditional singing of "Take Me Out to the Ball Game" during the seventh-inning stretch.

Cubs right fielder Sammy Sosa watches his sixty-first home run of the season leave Wrigley Field on September 13, 1998.

Caray passed away just before the 1998 season. The players honored him by wearing patches of his smiling face on their sleeves. Then Chicago embarked on a magical summer.

On May 6, Kerry Wood, a 20-year-old right-hander, offered a sign that new heroes were on the way. He tied an MLB record by striking out 20 Houston Astros in one game.

In June right fielder Sammy Sosa started grabbing headlines. He hit two home runs on June 1. By July 1 he had added 18 more, an MLB record for most home runs in a single month. That brought his season total to 33. As the summer went on, Sosa kept hitting homers. Yet so did St. Louis Cardinals first baseman Mark McGwire. Baseball fans grew more and more captivated as the sluggers closed in on the single-season record of 61 home runs. Both players broke it, but McGwire finished with 70 to Sosa's 66. The record chase made great entertainment. But the memories of the players' accomplishments were later tainted. Both Sosa and McGwire were accused of using performance-enhancing drugs (PEDs).

Sosa was still named NL MVP. And his enthusiasm for the game reminded some Cub fans of Banks. The slugger became Chicago's darling as he led the Cubs to the playoffs. But once again, the team came up short. The Atlanta Braves stopped the Cubs 3–0 in the NL Division Series (NLDS). The Cubs' wait for a championship had reached 90 years.

CHAPTER 4

THE CURSE BREAKERS

After winning only 65 games in 2000, the Cubs drafted a young right-handed pitcher named Mark Prior. He was billed as a surefire star. Prior joined the team in 2002 and was instantly one of MLB's best pitchers. The next year, he teamed with Kerry Wood, and Chicago's pitching staff was one of the NL's best.

The lineup also still included Sammy Sosa, plus other veterans such as third baseman Aramis Ramirez and left fielder Moisés Alou. The Cubs finished 88–74 and won their division for the first time since 1989. Then they shocked the Atlanta Braves by winning the NLDS. It was the team's first playoff series win since 1908.

Mark Prior won 18 games and struck out 245 batters for the Cubs in 2003.

Cubs fan Steve Bartman (in black) interferes with Chicago outfielder Moisés Alou's attempt to catch a foul pop in Game 6 of the 2003 NLCS.

The Cubs faced another surprising team, the Florida Marlins, in the NLCS. It was a close series, but the Cubs had a 3–2 lead going into Game 6 at Wrigley Field. Prior spent the game mowing down Florida hitters, allowing just three hits in seven innings. He got the first out in the eighth. With just five more outs, the Cubs would be headed to the World Series. But then the Marlins' Juan Pierre hit a double. Next up was second baseman Luis Castillo.

On a 3–2 count, Castillo hit a foul pop down the left-field line. Alou raced over to catch it near the first row of seats. Several fans reached up to grab it at the same moment as Alou. The ball bounced off the hands of a fan named Steve Bartman and fell to the ground. Alou reacted with anger. So did the fans around Bartman.

After the incident, everything fell apart for Chicago on the field. Prior allowed five runs as Florida tied the game. Then Cubs relievers gave up three more. The Cubs lost 8–3.

The series wasn't over. The Cubs had another chance to

BLOW UP THE CURSE

After the collapse against Florida, the manager of a Chicago restaurant purchased the infamous ball that Steve Bartman had interfered with. It was placed in a clear box and fed an electrical charge until the ball exploded. The idea was that destroying the ball would break the curse that seemed to hang over the Cubs.

win Game 7. They took a 5–3 lead but then fell apart in a 9–6 defeat.

Most fans felt that with a strong team, the Cubs would bounce back from their most devastating result yet. But those Cubs never got close to the World Series again. Prior was out of MLB four years later after an arm injury wrecked his career. The Cubs slowly dropped in the standings.

BATTLING THE CURSE

After the 2011 season, Chicago hired a new team president. Theo Epstein knew a thing or two about cursed baseball teams. He had built the 2004 Boston Red Sox squad that won that team's first World Series in 86 years.

Epstein focused on building long-term success. The Cubs struggled initially. They lost 101 games in 2012. However, Chicago was building a core of young talent through trades and the draft. Shortstop Javier Báez was the team's first draft pick in 2011. The Cubs traded for power hitting first baseman Anthony Rizzo in 2012. Third baseman Kris Bryant was the team's top pick in 2013.

The moves paid off in 2016. The Cubs blasted their way to 103 wins. Bryant was MVP. Rizzo hit 32 home runs. Starting pitchers Jon Lester, Jake Arrieta, and Kyle Hendricks anchored a deep pitching staff alongside flamethrowing closer Aroldis

Right-hander Jake Arrieta won the Cy Young Award in 2015 and helped anchor the Cubs' championship-winning pitching staff a year later.

Chapman. They marched past the Giants in the NLDS, then beat the Los Angeles Dodgers in the NLCS. The Cubs were back in the World Series for the first time since 1945.

MONUMENTAL COMEBACK

After four games of the World Series against Cleveland, Chicago fans wondered if their old luck had popped up again. Cleveland had a 3–1 lead. Then the Cubs eked out a 3–2 win in Game 5 to stay afloat. In Game 6, Chicago blew out Cleveland 9–3. Bryant and Rizzo combined for seven hits. Suddenly, the Cubs were one win away from breaking the 108-year streak.

Kris Bryant's first-inning home run spurred the Cubs to a 9–3 victory in Game 6 of the 2016 World Series, setting up the dramatic final game.

Late in Game 7, the Cubs seemed to be collapsing, just as they had so many times before. After holding a 5–1 lead, Chicago allowed Cleveland back in the game. Chapman gave up a surprising game-tying home run to light-hitting Cleveland outfielder Rajai Davis in the eighth inning.

The game was about to enter extra innings when a flash storm blew through Cleveland. The 17-minute delay helped the Cubs reset after veteran outfielder Jason Heyward gave his motivational speech to the team.

Chicago designated hitter Kyle Schwarber led off the 10th inning with a single. The speedy Albert Almora came in to run for him. Bryant then stepped to the plate. He hit a soaring fly ball out to center field. When the center fielder caught it, Almora took off for second base to get into scoring position.

Cubs players celebrate the team's first World Series victory in 108 years after beating Cleveland in 2016.

Cleveland chose to walk Rizzo and face Ben Zobrist, who was 0-for-4 on the night. Zobrist fell behind 1–2. But he got a pitch he could handle and shot it down the left-field line. Almora scored easily as Zobrist raced to second. Two batters later, Cubs catcher Miguel Montero hit a single to score Zobrist.

Needing just three more outs to break the 108-year curse, pitcher Carl Edwards Jr. struggled in the bottom of the 10th. He allowed a walk and a single that scored a run. With the tying run on first, left-hander Mike Montgomery came in and got a ground ball. Bryant scooped the slow roller and tossed it to Rizzo for the out. Cubs players touched off a wild celebration, as did their fans around the world. The wait was finally over. The Cubs were lovable losers no more.

AFTER THE BREAKTHROUGH

Bryant was 24 in 2016, while Báez was 23 and Rizzo was 26. They were just a few of the Cubs' young stars. Many around baseball expected the Cubs to build a dynasty. And while the Cubs reached the playoffs three of the next four seasons, they did not reach the World Series again.

In 2021 the Cubs began to take apart their championship core. Schwarber was already gone. Rizzo and Báez were both traded in July. The Cubs finished 71–91. Bryant left as a free agent after the season.

The Cubs signed Japanese star Seiya Suzuki before the 2022 season.

By 2022 just a few World Series winners were left on Chicago's roster. As the team made moves to build another contender, fans waited and hoped the rebuild would be a quick one. But Cubs fans were used to waiting and believing in their team.

TIMELINE

1876
The Chicago White Stockings join the National League and win the first league championship.

1886
The White Stockings win their sixth NL title in 10 years.

1902
After cycling through several nicknames, the White Stockings are referred to as the Cubs for the first time.

1906
The Cubs play in their first World Series, losing to the crosstown White Sox.

1907
The Cubs win their first World Series in a four-game sweep of the Detroit Tigers.

1908
The Cubs repeat as World Series champions, winning in five games over the Tigers.

1916
The Cubs move into Weeghman Park, now known as Wrigley Field.

1929
The Cubs win the National League for the first time in 11 years but lose the World Series 4–1 to the Philadelphia Athletics.

1930
Cubs outfielder Hack Wilson sets an MLB record with 191 RBIs.

1932

The Cubs reach the World Series again but fall to the New York Yankees in four games after Babe Ruth's famous "called shot" in Game 3.

1945

The Cubs lose the World Series to the Tigers as "the Curse of the Billy Goat" is born.

1959

"Mr. Cub" Ernie Banks wins his second consecutive NL MVP.

1969

After leading the division for much of the year, the Cubs collapse in September and finish eight games behind the New York Mets.

1984

In their first playoff series since 1945, the Cubs blow a 2–1 lead in the NLCS and lose to the San Diego Padres.

1989

The Cubs reach the NLCS but lose in five games to the San Francisco Giants.

1998

Sammy Sosa slugs 66 home runs as the Cubs win the NL wild card.

2003

Chicago loses the NLCS in seven games to the Florida Marlins after a late-inning collapse in Game 6.

2016

After a record 108 years without a championship, the Cubs defeat Cleveland in seven games to win the World Series.

TEAM FACTS

FRANCHISE HISTORY

Chicago White Stockings
(1876–89)
Chicago Colts (1890–97)
Chicago Orphans (1898–1902)
Chicago Cubs (1903–)

WORLD SERIES CHAMPIONSHIPS

1907, 1908, 2016

KEY PLAYERS

Cap Anson (1876–97)
Ernie Banks (1953–71)
Mordecai Brown
(1904–12, 1916)
Kris Bryant (2015–21)
Frank Chance (1898–1912)
Johnny Evers (1902–13)
Mark Grace (1988–2000)
Gabby Hartnett (1922–40)
Ferguson Jenkins (1966–73,
1982–83)
Mark Prior (2002–06)
Anthony Rizzo (2012–21)
Ryne Sandberg (1982–94,
1996–97)
Ron Santo (1960–73)
Sammy Sosa (1992–2004)
Joe Tinker (1902–12)
Hack Wilson (1926–31)
Kerry Wood (1998–2008,
2011–12)

KEY MANAGERS

Cap Anson (1880–97)
Frank Chance (1905–12)
Joe Maddon (2015–19)

HOME STADIUMS

23rd Street Grounds (1876–77)
Lakefront Park I (1878–82)
Lakefront Park II (1883–84)
West Side Park (1885–91)
South Side Park (1891–93)
West Side Grounds (1893–1915)
Wrigley Field (1916–)
Also known as:
Weeghman Park (1916–18)
Cubs Park (1919–26)

TEAM TRIVIA

TEAM DISCOUNT?

Former Cubs pitcher and later owner Al Spalding was the founder of the Spalding sporting goods company. Spalding created the first official MLB ball. The company also created the first football and basketball ever made.

SPRING FEVER

Cap Anson's White Stockings held one of baseball's first spring trainings in 1886, when Anson took 14 of his players to Hot Springs, Arkansas, to practice before the season.

SPRING FEVER, PART II

While the Cubs hold spring training today in Arizona, they have held it in many different locations over the years. The most unusual one was on Catalina Island off the coast of California. The Cubs held spring training there on and off from 1922 to 1951.

HACK GETS ONE BACK

Until 1999 Hack Wilson's single-season RBI record was thought to be 190. But eagle-eyed baseball historian Jerome Holtzman found one that was not counted properly from a doubleheader on July 28, 1930. The missing RBI was added on 69 years after Wilson's historic season.

GLOSSARY

ace

A team's best starting pitcher.

bleachers

Low-priced seating area for fans beyond the outfield fences.

closer

A pitcher who comes in at the end of the game to secure a win for his team.

draft

A system that allows teams to acquire new players coming into a league.

dynasty

A team that has an extended period of success, usually winning multiple championships in the process.

free agent

A player whose rights are not owned by any team.

general manager

An executive who runs a team and is responsible for finding and signing players.

seventh-inning stretch

The break between the top and bottom halves of the seventh inning, when fans traditionally sing "Take Me Out to the Ball Game."

shutout

A game in which a team does not score a single run.

sweep

Winning every game in a series.

MORE INFORMATION

BOOKS

Flynn, Brendan. *The MLB Encyclopedia*. Minneapolis, MN: Abdo Publishing, 2022.

Hewson, Anthony K. *GOATs of Baseball*. Minneapolis, MN: Abdo Publishing, 2022.

Mitchell, Bo. *Ultimate MLB Road Trip*. Minneapolis, MN: Abdo Publishing, 2019.

ONLINE RESOURCES

Booklinks
NONFICTION NETWORK
FREE! ONLINE NONFICTION RESOURCES

To learn more about the Chicago Cubs, please visit **abdobooklinks.com** or scan this QR code. These links are routinely monitored and updated to provide the most current information available.

INDEX

ABOUT THE AUTHOR

Anthony K. Hewson is a freelance writer originally from San Diego. He and his wife now live in the San Francisco Bay Area with their two dogs.